Grace Like Wildflowers

Grandma Floe,

Thank you for being my best friend for 31 years and always loving me like Jesus. I love you to the moon and back. C U Later.

Grandma Hampton,

I will never be as cool as you, but I will always be grateful for the 10 years that I was loved by you. Thank you for the gift of your love and for sharing your family with me.

Grace Like Wildflowers

30 DAY DEVOTIONAL
FOR A FLOURISHING SOUL

Emily Hampton

Grace Like Wildflowers by Emily Hampton

Published by: ADVANTAGE BOOKS™
Longwood, FL. www.advbookstore.com

Scripture quotations are taken from The Holy Bible, New Living Translation (NLT), copyright© 1996, 2004, 2015 by Tyndale House Foundation. Used by permission of Tyndale House Publishers, Carol Stream, Illinois 60188. All rights reserved.

Library of Congress Catalog Number: 2024945495

Name:	Hampton, Emily Author
Title:	*Grace Like Wildflowers: A 30 Day Devotional for a Flourishing Soul*
	Emily Hampton
	Advantage Books, 2024
Identifiers:	ISBN Paperback: 9781597558075
	ISBN eBook: 9781597558181
Subjects:	RELIGION: Christian Life – Devotional
	RELIGION: Christian Life – Inspirational
	RELIGION: Christian Life – Spiritual Growth

First Printing: September 2024
24 25 26 27 28 29 30   10 9 8 7 6 5 4 3 2 1

Lord,

I pray You would give me the words to fill the pages of this book and therefore fill the hearts of those who will read it. I pray this book would be a vessel of Your word, a light in this world, and an anchor connecting us to You. This book is not for my glory, but for Yours. The credit is Yours. Guide me. Protect my heart and mind. Ultimately, use this book for Your good and to further Your kingdom here on earth.

Amen.

Emily Hampton

Grace Like Wildflowers

Introduction

Welcome to "Grace Like Wildflowers: A 30-Day Devotional for a Flourishing Soul." I'm delighted to have you join me on this transformative journey where we'll explore the vibrant theme of grace that blooms in our lives like wildflowers. Just as wildflowers flourish in unexpected places, God's grace has the power to bring beauty to every corner of our existence.

In the next 30 days, let's reflect on the ways God's grace has unfolded in the various seasons of our lives. Much like wildflowers that thrive in diverse landscapes, God's grace meets us wherever we are, bringing color and vibrancy to our souls.

This devotional is more than a daily reading; it's an invitation to embrace the wild and untamed grace God offers. Together, let's navigate the terrain of grace, allowing it to cultivate a flourishing soul within us. Let each day bring you closer to the beauty of God's grace, transforming your heart and soul like wildflowers in full bloom.

Emily Hampton

Day 1: Introduction to Grace

Scripture:

Ephesians 2:8 (NLT): "God saved you by His grace when you believed. And you can't take credit for this; it is a gift from God."

Reflection

GRACE. The foundation of my faith journey is built upon it. I did not come into a relationship with Jesus until I was an adult. I'm sure you can imagine some of the things I got into before knowing Jesus. I lived for the next party, the next relationship—ultimately, I lived for myself and whatever thing brought temporary "happiness" into my life at that moment. I believe this is why grace is so very important to me—I have experienced firsthand how it changes everything. In fact, without the transformative power of God's grace breaking into my life, I doubt I'd be where I am today, embracing grace and striving to live the fulfilling life He has envisioned for me. Living for Jesus requires our daily recommitment because, let's face it, even if we get it right one day, we might mess up the next. But His grace and love remain constant, ever ready to lift us up and guide us forward. I NEEDED God's grace in order to accept His unconditional love for me for the first time and I recognize how much I still need it today. My baptism is not the most pivotal moment of my walk with Jesus. It came long before that when I fell to my knees in my bathroom and repented of all I had done in my life leading to that moment. I felt completely new—as if His grace washed away every single poor choice I ever made in my life.

Devotional Message

The thing about grace is this: we don't deserve it, and yet, God freely gives it to us. Jesus came into this world as a human being. He alone is sinless and fully understands the challenges we face every single day on this Earth. The only thing He requires of us is our belief in Him and our pure-hearted love for Him. That's it! His grace is a gift to us. But like all gifts—we have to actively receive it.

Have you ever given someone a gift, and they said, "No, it's too much, I can't accept this"? I am an avid lover of gift-giving, and if someone didn't accept my gift, I would be crushed! But if we didn't want to give that gift, we wouldn't have! That's how it is with God's gift of grace. He wants us to joyfully accept it and fully bask in it. He wants us to thank Him for it and cherish it every single day.

And when we do—everything changes.

Reflective Question

Imagine how your life might be transformed if you completely accepted God's gift of grace. What might change? Might you feel less guilt and shame? Might you feel freer to live the life He intended for you? Take a moment to journal your reflections. Consider writing down your thoughts and feelings as you contemplate the transformative power of God's grace in your life.

Prayer

Lord, thank You that Your grace is abundantly mine. I pray I would fully accept the gift of grace You have freely given me. Help me explore the parts of my heart that have not yet given in to Your grace. Help me understand the vastness of Your grace and walk in it daily.

Notes

_____

_____

_____

_____

Day 2: Embracing Boundless Grace

Scripture

Romans 11:6 (NLT): "And since it is through God's kindness, then it is not by their good works. For in that case, God's grace would not be what it really is - free and undeserved."

Reflection

Free and undeserved. This verse says it all! It shows us we cannot earn God's grace. We cannot work to be "good" enough for it or complete a checklist and finally receive it. It is free. That takes some of the pressure off doesn't it? From the time we take our first breath, His boundless grace is ours.

Devotional Message

God has way more grace for us than we have for ourselves. Those unkind thoughts and feelings you have towards yourself? That is NOT God. We are human beings. We are sinful by nature. We should ALWAYS strive to be more like Jesus, but we are mere mortals! No one is perfect 100% of the time. And when we do miss the mark (when, not if) we are covered by His grace. When I first became a mom I would lie in bed at night and run through all of the ways I fell short that day. (I didn't play with my son enough; the house was a mess and I didn't get around to cleaning it; I wasn't as patient as I should have been when I was tired and overwhelmed). It took me an embarrassingly long time to realize I was basking in lies from the enemy, not in truth and grace from God! I started trying to see myself as He sees me-a human being trying my best to love Him and those around me and that changed everything. He is a good, kind, loving, understanding Father. In His grace, we find freedom and have permission to fully walk in it.

Reflective Question

Think of a time you felt you missed the mark. What did you think of yourself at that time? Does that align with what God says about you (that you are LOVED deeply, that you are HIS daughter/son, that He created you in His image)? Grab a journal or use the space provided in this book to record your reflections on today's devotional. Write down your thoughts, feelings, and any insights that come to you. Feel free to revisit these reflections as you continue this 30-day journey. Your personal growth is an integral part of our shared exploration of God's grace.

Prayer

Lord, help me have as much grace for myself as You have for me. Help me see myself as You do - as a beloved child of God. Lord help me live a sinless life, but fully walk in the grace You have for me when I fall short. I repent for the times I missed the mark. Thank You for unconditional love and forgiveness whether I have sinned one time or hundreds. Thank You for Your free and undeserved grace. Guide me in recognizing Your kindness in everyday moments.

Notes

_____

_____

_____

_____

_____

_____

_____

_____

Day 3: Grace and Love

Scripture

1 John 4:16 (NLT): "We know how much God loves us, and we have put our trust in His love. God is love, and all who live in love live in God, and God lives in them."

Reflection

We can't talk about grace without talking about love. He has grace for us BECAUSE He loves us. Have you ever met parents who believe their children can do no wrong? They have blind spots to their children's wrongdoings because they love them so much it is hard to imagine they are less than perfect (even though we all are). It isn't like that with God- there are no blind spots in His love for us. He sees us fully (the good, the bad and the ugly) and He loves us uncontrollably anyways!

Devotional Message

When I was 6 years old (and having a very bad day) I karate chopped my grandma in the knee. Honestly, 26 years later it is still hard for me to own up to that. My grandma was my absolute best friend and one of the most loving people on this Earth…and I karate chopped her. But you know what? My grandma loved me so much that she said, "Emily, I am not mad at you. You are a sweet little girl and I love you very much." Did I mention I had JUST karate chopped her? I honestly believe her response in that situation is the perfect reflection of God's love and grace for us. When we fall short, He does not respond in anger. He responds in grace and love-every single time. God's unconditional love, without blind spots, is the foundation for His unmerited grace.

Reflective Question

Think of a time you clearly fell short (maybe not karate-chop-your-grandma fall short but still). How did the person experiencing you in that moment respond? If their response was not Jesus-like, how could they have responded differently?

Prayer

Lord, thank You for Your all seeing, all accepting love for us. Thank You for responding in grace when we miss the mark. I pray for a deeper understanding of Your love. Please help me extend Your love and grace to every person and in every situation in my life.

Notes

_____

_____

_____

_____

_____

_____

_____

_____

_____

_____

_____

_____

Day 4: The Transformative Power of Grace

Scripture

2 Corinthians 12:9 (NLT): "Each time He said, 'My grace is all you need. My power works best in weakness.' So now I am glad to boast about my weaknesses, so the power of Christ can work through me."

Reflection

"My grace is all you need." Take a moment and let that fully sink in. We throw around the word "need" a bit carelessly in our culture. I NEED more clothes; I NEED a bigger TV; I NEED an overpriced workout bike; you name it (or advertise it well enough) and I need it. What if we truly believed the only thing we needed was His grace? What if that was enough to get us through each moment? Some of the hardest times in my life have been the moments when I experienced God's grace and love in the most real, life changing ways. In fact, when feeling far from Him I reflect to those pivotal moments to remember He is crazy about me and wants to show up in every single moment, in every season of my life.

Devotional Message

Unfortunately, like many of you who read this, I had a miscarriage several years ago. Talk about being weak. But you know what? God used even something as heart wrenching as that experience was to show me how much He truly loves me. I honestly have a hard time finding the words to convey the ways I experienced Him during one of the saddest times of my life. I was so open to hearing from Him and seeing Him in those moments I experienced Him in everything. I even sensed Him comforting me and telling me, "You will get another chance." Because I was desperate and weak-I searched for Him. I longed for His peace and grace so much I saw it everywhere I looked. I truly felt His comfort. But before any of that, I had to first acknowledge my weakness. I had to admit I couldn't get through it alone. When I embraced my vulnerability it led to a profound transformation through God's grace.

Reflective Question

Life is hard. In fact, I am sure you are walking through something hard right now. Take a moment to reflect on and acknowledge a weakness in your life right at this moment. What can you do to hand this off to God a little bit more today? Can you journal about it? Talk to a trusted friend about it? Ask a fellow Christ-follower for prayer? There is healing power in vulnerability which leads to transformation in Jesus.

Prayer

Lord, we acknowledge that life can be hard and we recognize we cannot do it alone. Thank You for Your transformative peace and presence in these challenging, heart-wrenching circumstances. I pray Your grace would truly be enough for me and for the strength to boast in my weaknesses, allowing the power of Christ to work through every aspect of life.

Notes

_____

_____

_____

_____

_____

_____

_____

Day 5: Grace Beyond Mistakes

Scripture

Romans 8:1 (NLT): So now there is no condemnation for those who belong to Christ Jesus.

Reflection

Mistakes are an unavoidable part of our journey. We are taught this lesson from the time we are children learning to play well with others! I've echoed this countless times to my own children. We all make mistakes - that's undeniable. Yet, the true power lies in our response to those mistakes. Do we succumb to self-blame and let frustration spill onto those around us? Or do we embrace the reality of our existence in a broken world, acknowledging our humanity and choosing to walk in the truth and freedom found in receiving His forgiveness and grace?

Devotional Message

If we never made mistakes, we wouldn't need God's grace. If we were perfect and lived in a flawless world, we wouldn't need to rely on God - in fact, we may miss out on a relationship with Him altogether. God's grace doesn't just cover our mistakes - it removes them completely. This means we don't have to hold onto them and continue to beat ourselves up over them.

Picture This

It was a sunny afternoon, and I was attempting a majestic parking maneuver in our driveway (A.K.A. I was simply trying to park in our driveway). In the midst of parking, a not-so-graceful moment occurred—I sideswiped our mailbox, leaving an undeniable scratch on our car. Rather than trying to hide my mistake out of shame and embarrassment, I decided to face the music. I immediately confessed my accident to my husband. Instead of a scowl or frustration, he responded with a gentle smile and an understanding nod. He assured me it was okay, that accidents happen, and the scratch was just a small blemish in the grand scheme of things.

What if this is how we approached our mistakes—big or small—with God? Just as my husband reassured me with love and gentleness, God, in His infinite grace, reminds us that our mistakes are just small blemishes in the grand scheme of His plan. What if our first response was to confess through prayer and immediately reap the benefits of His grace: forgiveness, freedom, connection, and understanding? The mistakes we won't let go of take up space in our hearts, leaving less room for Jesus.

Reflective Question

Think of a mistake or blunder that still lingers in your memory (big or small). How might embracing the concept of grace beyond mistakes bring healing and freedom to both that moment and the present? Consider the power of forgiveness, both in receiving it for you and extending it to others.

Prayer

Lord, thank You for seeing us as more than the mistakes we have made. I repent for the times I have messed up. I am so thankful that in You, I am made new and washed completely clean. Please give me the strength to let go of any resounding guilt and shame I have in my heart, embracing the freedom offered to me through Your unending forgiveness.

Notes

_____

_____

_____

Day 6: Gratitude amidst Grief

Scripture

1 Thessalonians 5:18 (NLT): "Be thankful in all circumstances, for this is God's will for you who belong to Christ Jesus."

Reflection

Have you ever listened to the song "I'm Thankful for the Scars" by I Am They? If not, it's worth a moment to take a listen. The lyrics resonate deeply: "I'm thankful for the scars 'Cause without them I wouldn't know Your heart. And I know they'll always tell of who You are." Being thankful during painful moments can be incredibly challenging, yet I believe that's exactly what God calls us to do. Our times of pain are opportunities to experience God in His full glory. He desires to show up for us, offering comfort and transforming our perspective if we allow Him to do so. In those moments, we can encounter God like never before.

Devotional Message

You know, I wasn't planning to talk about this in this devotional—it's too soon, too real, too raw. But the more I pray about it, the more I feel called to share what I am currently walking through. About two weeks before starting this devotional, my Grandma Floe passed away. And just three weeks before that, my husband's Grandma Helen passed away. Yet, even in the midst of this grief, I feel it's necessary to talk about being thankful in all circumstances.

The only reason I can do that is because I have experienced God's grace, love, and presence so profoundly over the past month that I literally cannot keep it in anymore. I have to tell the world how purely, completely, and passionately He loves His children. While this has been one of the most challenging months of my life, I am beyond grateful for His love and grace.

During this time, I found myself completely drained, emotionally and physically. There were moments when I didn't think I could get out of bed, let alone stand up at my grandma's funeral and speak about her life. But it was in those very moments of weakness that I felt God's strength the most. I would pray, sometimes with nothing more than tears, and He would meet me there. His presence became my source of strength, helping me do what I couldn't do on my own. He gave me the courage to stand before my family and honor my grandma, even when I felt like I had nothing left to give.

This experience taught me that His strength is made perfect in our weakness (2 Corinthians 12:9). When we come to the end of our own abilities, that's when we can truly lean on Him. And the beautiful thing is that He is always ready to carry us, no matter how heavy the burden. We don't have to face our struggles alone. Just as He was with me during my deepest grief, He is with you, ready to lend you His strength.

So, in every single circumstance, we can find SOMETHING—even if it is only one thing—to be grateful for. And one of the greatest gifts we can be thankful for is the strength He provides when ours isn't enough. Of that, I am certain.

Reflective Question

In challenging moments, have you experienced a glimpse of God's grace that shifted your perspective toward gratitude? Reflect on a specific instance where gratitude emerged, even in difficulty, and consider how that moment transformed your relationship with God.

Prayer

Lord, I do thank You for the scars on my heart. I thank You for every single time You showed up for me, whether I acknowledged You or not. I am exceedingly grateful You have never, not even for a moment, left my side and that You never will. I pray for Your grace to cover me and that You would help my heart be thankful in all circumstances.

Notes

_____

_____

_____

_____

_____

_____

_____

_____

_____

_____

_____

_____

_____

_____

_____

_____

_____

_____

_____

_____

_____

Emily Hampton

Day 7: Everyday Offerings of Love

Scripture

Psalm 116:12 (NLT) - "What can I offer the Lord for all He has done for me?"

Luke 10:41-42 (NLT) - "But the Lord said to her, 'My dear Martha, you are worried and upset over all these details! There is only one thing worth being concerned about. Mary has discovered it, and it will not be taken away from her.'"

Reflection

This morning, my two little boys brought me gifts—ice cream paintings they had made a while back. Even though they were gifts I had already received, they brought sincere joy to my heart. It wasn't about the value or the skill behind them; it was about their thoughtful hearts wanting to delight me. Similarly, when Mary chose to sit at Jesus' feet rather than busy herself with tasks, she offered Him something simple yet profound: her presence.

In our daily lives, God invites us to present our own offerings—simple acts of love, gratitude, and surrender. These offerings, like Mary's attentive presence and my children's paintings, might not be grand, but it's the sincerity behind them that delights God's heart.

Devotional Message

The everyday offerings we bring to God don't need to be grand gestures; they can be as simple as a few moments in prayer, acts of kindness, time in His Word, or just sitting quietly at His feet, as Mary did. In Psalm 116:12, the psalmist wonders what can be offered to the Lord for all He has done. Just like Martha, we can get caught up in the details of life, but God doesn't require us to repay

Him. Instead, He desires our sincere hearts, just as Jesus treasured Mary's presence over busyness.

Our actions, no matter how small, become brushstrokes on the canvas of our faith, creating a beautiful masterpiece of love in response to His continuous grace.

Reflective Question

How can you be more like Mary today, offering your presence to God? What simple, everyday offerings of love can you bring before Him, reflecting your gratitude for His unmerited grace?

Prayer

Lord, guide us in recognizing the beauty in our everyday offerings; may our acts of love, no matter how small, be a sweet gift to You. Thank You for Your unmerited grace, prompting our hearts to respond in love.

Notes

_____

_____

_____

_____

_____

_____

_____

_____

_____

Day 8: Sustained by Grace

Scripture

Psalm 145:15-16 (NLT) - "The eyes of all look to You, and You give them their food at the proper time. You open Your hand and satisfy the desires of every living thing."

Reflection

What does it really mean to be satisfied? I can't count the times I've tried to fill the empty spaces in my heart with material things. It took me a long time to realize that true satisfaction can't be bought at Target or on Amazon—it comes from God alone. In the dance of life, God's grace is our constant sustenance. Like a reliable stream, it flows endlessly, providing the nourishment we need for every step of our journey.

Devotional Message

The most amazing part is this: God's grace isn't a one-time gift—it's a continuous outpouring that sustains us through every moment and every season of our lives. It's the ever-present hand that feeds our souls, satisfies our longings, and ensures we lack nothing. Does that mean we'll get everything we want when we want it? Of course not. But it does mean we can trust that God's plans for our lives go far beyond anything we can imagine.

As someone who's grown a garden, I know firsthand how all-consuming it is to pour love into living things. Any lapse in care can lead to disastrous consequences (just ask my poor garden from 2022, when we left it for a week to go to the beach!). In our fast-paced lives, it's easy to overlook the steady stream of God's grace. Take a moment today to recognize how constantly He provides for you. Just as a garden flourishes when tended to regularly, our spirits thrive when we're immersed in the constant grace of our Heavenly Gardener.

One way to stay connected to this constant grace is to set aside a few moments each day to simply acknowledge God's presence in your life. It could be as simple as pausing in the morning to thank Him for a new day, or whispering a prayer of gratitude in the middle of a hectic afternoon. When we intentionally focus on His goodness, even in small ways, we create space for His grace to fill our hearts and satisfy our deepest needs.

So, let's take comfort in that reassurance, fully resting in the knowledge that He won't ever take a vacation from us!

Reflective Question

How can you actively acknowledge and appreciate the constant grace that sustains you daily?

Prayer

Lord, thank You for the unceasing flow of Your grace that sustains me. Help me cultivate an awareness of Your constant provision in my life; may I be attuned to the rhythms of Your grace, finding strength and nourishment in every moment. Amen.

Notes

_____

_____

_____

_____

_____

_____

Day 9: God's Relentless Guidance and Comfort

Scripture

Proverbs 3: 5-6 (NLT):Trust in the Lord with all your heart; do not depend on your own understanding. Seek His will in all you do, and He will show you which path to take.

Reflection

When I got pregnant with Max, my second son, I knew I would need an abundance of God's grace to navigate the journey. Having previously experienced a miscarriage, every little twinge and pain triggered anxiety. Early on, I realized the importance of entrusting my pregnancy to God, leaning on His grace for the months ahead. The fear and uncertainty of pregnancy after loss can be overwhelming, but God's guidance and comfort became a beacon of hope. It wasn't until I fully surrendered my fears to Him (sometimes multiple times a day) and asked my friends to pray for me and my unborn baby that I could truly embrace the journey of pregnancy, savoring each magical moment as a gift from God.

Devotional Message

When I first learned I was pregnant, I was genuinely terrified. Despite the excitement of a planned pregnancy, fear gripped me. It dawned on me that I was relying on my own understanding rather than God's. My past pain and trauma had a way of sneaking into the present. But God already knew the outcome of my pregnancy, and I realized that no amount of worrying would change that. As I shifted my focus to seek His will and not my own, everything changed. God freed me from the chains of anxiety, guiding me to fix my eyes on Him. I learned to trust that He would be with me, regardless of the circumstances, and that His plans for my life were beyond my control.

It's worth mentioning that my pregnancy turned out to be high-risk, requiring twice as many checkups and ultrasounds as usual. Surprisingly, instead of causing fear, it actually calmed my anxiety because of the close monitoring I received. Complete trust in God can be challenging, and it isn't a one-time decision to hand over our fears. It requires daily, sometimes multiple times a day, reliance on God. The freedom of allowing God to carry our burdens for us is unparalleled.

Whatever it is you're walking through—whether it's big or small, a season of joy or a season of struggle—know that God wants to be your guiding light, your rock, and your constant source of strength. Just as He walked with me through my fears and uncertainties, He's ready to walk with you through yours. When we earnestly seek His will and lean on Him, not only does He illuminate our path, but He also walks beside us, revealing His presence in ways we never thought possible.

Reflective Question

Have you experienced God's guidance and comfort in a challenging season? Reflect on those moments and thank Him for His sustaining grace.

Prayer

God, we thank You that You are an ever present, ever loving God. We thank You that You are truly in control and You have our story written in advance. Thank You for Your guidance and comfort, especially in times of uncertainty and fear.

Notes

_____

_____

_____

Day 10: Finding Peace amidst COVID Anxiety

Scripture

Philippians 4:6-7: Don't worry about anything; instead, pray about everything. Tell God what you need, and thank Him for all He has done. Then you will experience God's peace, which exceeds anything we can understand. His peace will guard your hearts and minds as you live in Christ Jesus.

Reflection

I initially hesitated to write about Covid in my book, but as I reflected on the most challenging seasons of my life, that period certainly stood out. Becoming a new mom during the pandemic added layers of anxiety I hadn't known before. Stories of babies facing health crises and the isolation from friends and family only heightened the stress. It was an unprecedented time for everyone, and no one knew what the future held. We were cut off from our support systems, and the need for God's grace and peace became more apparent than ever.

Devotional Message

The challenges of Covid brought fear and anxiety into the lives of many, myself included. In those uncertain times, the only thing that brought me solace was drawing closer to God. His Word became a source of comfort, and worship music filled our home, bringing hope into the midst of chaos. As I look back on that season, I realize something profound: the moments of deepest struggle were also the sweetest times with the Lord.

In the midst of our vulnerabilities, we're often driven to rely more deeply on God's grace. It's in these moments of uncertainty that His presence becomes most tangible. The pandemic served as a crucible where our human fears collided with God's unshakeable love. With each anxious breath, I found assurance in His Word. What began as isolation turned into intimate encounters with God, teaching me that in life's storms, His grace is our anchor, and His Word is our guide.

No matter what challenges you're facing today—whether it's anxiety about the future, health concerns, or feelings of isolation— remember that God's peace is available to you. Just as He met me in my fears during the pandemic, He is ready to meet you in whatever you're walking through right now.

Here are some tangible ways you can begin to rely on God, even if you've never done so before:

1. **Start with Prayer:** Simply talk to God about what's on your mind. You don't need fancy words—just open your heart. Begin by thanking Him for even the smallest blessings, and then share your worries with Him.
2. **Read Scripture:** Spend a few minutes each day reading the Bible. Start with verses that speak about peace, such as Philippians 4:6-7, and meditate on them throughout the day. Let His promises replace your worries.
3. **Listen to Worship Music:** Fill your environment with worship music. Let the lyrics remind you of God's presence and His faithfulness. Music has a way of shifting our focus from our problems to His power.
4. **Join a Community:** If you feel isolated, consider joining a church group, Bible study, or even an online Christian community. Being around others who are also seeking God can provide support and encouragement.
5. **Practice Gratitude:** Each day, write down three things you're thankful for. This simple practice can help shift your perspective from what's lacking to what's abundant, making it easier to see God's hand in your life.
6. **Surrender Your Worries:** When anxiety creeps in, take a deep breath and consciously surrender your worries to God. Imagine placing them in His hands, knowing that He cares for you and is in control.

When we turn our worries into prayers and thank Him for all He has done, we open ourselves to experiencing His peace—a peace that goes beyond anything we can understand. Let this be a reminder to seek solace in worship, find strength in His promises, and allow uncertainties to deepen your trust in the One who holds everything in His hands.

Reflective Question

How have you sought peace in God's grace during times of anxiety, especially amidst the challenges of COVID?

Prayer

Lord, may Your profound peace govern our hearts. We acknowledge and cherish Your enduring and ever-present love. In the face of life's unforeseen challenges, we seek Your guidance and protection, grateful that nothing catches you by surprise.

Notes

_____

_____

_____

_____

_____

_____

_____

_____

_____

_____

_____

Emily Hampton

Day 11: Comfort before Acknowledgment

Scripture

Psalm 34:17-18: The LORD hears His people when they call to Him for help. He rescues them from all their troubles. The LORD is close to the brokenhearted; He rescues.

Reflection

As a child, like many of you reading this, I navigated my parents' divorce, which led to a move to a different state with my mom and sister. The longing for the part of my family left behind—my dad, brother, and grandma—was an indescribable ache. I distinctly recall one night, alone in our new house, tears streaming down my face as I was overwhelmed by a sense of hopelessness and profound loss.

Devotional Message

As I lay in my bed that night, nothing extraordinary happened that I was aware of. I was just a sad little girl grieving her family. But you know what? Several years later, when I began closely walking with Jesus, He painted a vivid picture of that night in my mind. The memory was as clear as day. He revealed to me an image of Himself sitting at the end of my bed, crying with me. His heart was broken because mine was broken. I realized then that I had never truly been alone for a single moment of my life—even before I fully acknowledged who He was. I was brokenhearted, and He was as close as He could be.

This revelation changed everything. It illuminated the truth that even in our darkest moments, God is intimately present, sharing our pain and offering His comfort. I often think back to that moment and am overwhelmed by His love for me. How many moments in my life, in your life, has God been actively comforting us, even when we didn't realize it? How many tears has He quietly wiped away in our most sorrowful times? How many times has He yearned for us to simply turn to Him, yet still, He stayed by our side, never leaving?

Reflective Question

Close your eyes and bring to mind a difficult time from your past. Now, imagine Jesus right there with you in that moment. Can you feel His presence? Take a moment to journal about a time when He was undoubtedly there, even if you couldn't see Him then. How does knowing this change the way you view that moment now?

Prayer

Lord, we thank You for Your unwavering presence in the midst of our challenges. As we reflect on difficult times, help us to see your comforting embrace and know we were never alone. Guide us in understanding how these moments have shaped our journey and drawn us closer to You. Amen.

Notes

_____

_____

_____

_____

_____

_____

_____

_____

_____

Day 12: God's Power in Small Openings

Scripture

Isaiah 43:19 For I am about to do something new. See, I have already begun! Do you not see it? I will make a pathway through the wilderness. I will create rivers.

Reflection

Today, I took my boys to an indoor playground filled with bouncy houses. As I sat back and observed them, I noticed how they eagerly squeezed through the tiny openings of the bounce houses to reach the insides. They pushed through with determination, and once inside, they were full of joy, experiencing the wonder of each bouncy house. It struck me that God often presents us with small openings, and by persistently and faithfully moving through them, we can discover the fullness of joy He has waiting for us.

Devotional Message

In our daily lives, God provides us with subtle openings, much like the small entrances to those bounce houses. These moments might come in unexpected ways: a brief encounter with a stranger who needs a smile, a chance to extend forgiveness to someone who's hurt us, or an opportunity to try something new that feels a bit intimidating. While they might seem insignificant, these small openings can lead to profound experiences and joy if we persistently and faithfully embrace them.

Consider something as simple as paying for the person behind you in the drive-thru. It's a small gesture, but it can spark a ripple effect. That person, touched by your kindness, might then do something kind for someone else, and the cycle of kindness continues, spreading joy far beyond that initial moment. You may never see the full impact of that single act, but God can use it to touch many lives.

Just as my children squeezed through those tiny entrances with excitement, let's approach the small openings God presents to us with anticipation and courage. Whether it's showing kindness to a stranger, embracing new challenges, or reaching out to someone who randomly comes to our mind, these openings can lead to the fullness of joy God desires for our lives.

And remember, each small step of faith we take can create a ripple effect. The kindness we show today might inspire others to do the same, creating waves of joy and grace that touch countless lives. May we remain attentive to His guidance and step through each small opening with faith and joy, trusting that He has something beautiful waiting on the other side.

Reflective Question

Be on the lookout for small openings today. How might you step through them with faith and discover the new things God has in store for you?

Prayer

Lord, help us recognize the significance of small openings in our lives. May we trust in Your transformative power, knowing even the smallest opportunities can lead to profound blessings. Give us the courage to see these small openings for what they are-a chance to experience the fullness of life You have for us. Amen.

Notes

_____

_____

_____

_____

_____

Day 13: Reflecting the Love of Our Heavenly Father

Scripture

Ephesians 5:1 - "Therefore be imitators of God, as beloved children."

Reflection

My husband is a Worship Leader, and he recently released his first album. Watching the music video on YouTube has been a HUGE deal for our boys! Today, as we were watching the video, my little ones ran to grab their drums and guitar, joyfully playing along with their dad on TV. In the simplicity of that moment, I was struck by a profound truth – the beauty of modeling our lives after the love and grace of our Heavenly Father. Seeing my boys imitate their dad became a powerful reminder of our journey as disciples of Christ.

Devotional Message

Just as children naturally imitate their parents, we are called to echo our Heavenly Father in our daily lives. My boys eagerly mimicking their dad's moves is a picture of how we should imitate Jesus in everything we do. Think about it – every action, challenge, and celebration is an opportunity to reflect the love and grace we've freely received.

Consider how joyful my little ones were as they played along with their dad. In the same way, when we choose to reflect God's love in our actions, we not only bring joy to ourselves but also to others. Our everyday choices – how we treat others, respond to difficulties, and celebrate successes – can become a beautiful dance, harmonizing with the rhythm of God's love and grace.

So today, as you go about your daily life, be intentional in echoing God's love. Let your actions resonate with His unfailing love. Whether it's offering a kind word to someone who needs it, showing patience in a stressful situation, or simply being present with a loved one, each moment is an opportunity to reflect His grace. The impact of your actions, however small they may seem, can create ripples of love and hope in the lives of others.

Reflective Question

How can you intentionally echo God's love in your actions today, creating a reflection of His grace? Think of one specific way you can imitate Him in your interactions, and make it a priority today.

Prayer

Lord, guide us as we seek to imitate Your boundless love; may our actions echo the grace we receive from You, creating a reflection of Your enduring love. Amen.

Notes

_____

_____

_____

_____

_____

_____

_____

_____

_____

_____

Day 14: The One True Fulfillment

Scripture

Psalm 73:26 - "My flesh and my heart may fail, but God is the strength of my heart and my portion forever."

Reflection

Before I knew Jesus, I tried to fill the void in my heart with parties, relationships, and material pursuits. I was on a relentless search for lasting joy, but nothing truly satisfied me until I encountered the unconditional love of Jesus. His love wasn't just another piece of the puzzle; it was the masterpiece that completed the canvas of my life, filling the Jesus-sized hole in my heart with profound contentment, purpose, and acceptance.

Devotional Message

As I look back, I realize that I'm not alone in trying to fill that void. Many of us turn to other things, hoping they will ease our pain, bring acceptance, peace, or joy. But here's the truth: these things can only provide temporary relief. I've personally struggled with turning to binge-watching shows, endlessly scrolling through social media, or picking up the phone to vent when someone offends me. It's a daily, moment-by-moment choice that I still have to make, and I'm far from perfect in this area.

But I've learned that instead of picking up the phone to call someone and vent, I can bow my head in prayer and take it to God. Instead of scrolling through social media (which almost always makes me feel worse, by the way), I can open my Bible and read through His promises. Instead of binge-watching Netflix, I can go outside and take a walk, marveling at His creation. God should be our ultimate security blanket—the one we wrap ourselves in when life gets tough.

It takes courage to name these things, to confront them—but this is a vital step in deepening your relationship with Jesus. This process may stir discomfort, but once we identify the things we rely on instead of God, we gain insight into when we lean on something other than the One who created us and promised to love us unconditionally.

These temporary fixes may distract us for a moment, but they can never truly satisfy the deep longing in our hearts. Let this revelation propel you into God's arms—He is the true and unwavering strength of our hearts. As we acknowledge our need for Him, we discover a fulfillment that no substitute can ever provide. When we embrace this truth and fully surrender to the loving arms of Jesus, we find not only solace but a profound and lasting peace that transcends our deepest yearnings.

Reflective question

Today, take a moment to reflect on the things you've been leaning on instead of God. Name them, confront them, and bring them before Jesus. Choose to wrap yourself in His love and grace, making Him your ultimate source of comfort and security. Trust that as you let go of those temporary fixes, you'll experience the deep and abiding peace that only He can offer.

Prayer

Lord, reveal to me the substitutes I've clung to, and grant me the courage to surrender them to You. I acknowledge that You alone are the true sustainer of my heart. In Your loving arms, I find solace and lasting peace. Amen.

Notes

_____

_____

Day 15: Not by My Strength, but His

Scripture

Philippians 4:13 - "I can do all things through Him who strengthens me."

Reflection

I started gymnastics at a young age, a sport I adored and aimed to excel in. Even before beginning, I envisioned mastering certain skills. However, in the initial stages, I was physically weak. Recognizing the need for strength to perform the desired tricks, I committed to gaining the necessary skills diligently. Over time, my efforts paid off, and I became increasingly stronger, achieving the once-dreamed-of skills. Similarly, as we consistently practice relying on, hearing from, and trusting Jesus, we develop spiritual muscles that make recognizing Him in everything much easier.

Devotional Message

Just as I trained my body in gymnastics through persistent practice, our spiritual journey with Jesus requires daily commitment and intentionality. Each day brings opportunities to lean on Him— whether it's managing stress, navigating relationships, or dealing with personal struggles. As we practice turning to Jesus in these moments, our spiritual muscles grow stronger, and we begin to see His presence in every part of our lives.

For example, instead of letting frustration build up after a challenging day, we can take a few minutes to journal our thoughts and pray for God's guidance. Or when we're feeling overwhelmed by our to-do list, we can pause and ask God for wisdom on what truly needs to be done, rather than pushing ourselves to exhaustion. These intentional choices help us to rely on Him more deeply.

The more we practice relying on Jesus, the more natural it

becomes—just like when I mastered gymnastics skills. I reached a point where I could perform complex tricks without even thinking about them. Imagine if seeking Jesus became that natural for us. Imagine starting each day with the intention of seeking Him in every aspect of your life and ending it by reflecting on where you saw Him at work throughout the day.

Reflective Question

Today, identify an area where you often rely on something other than Jesus—whether it's a habit, a distraction, or a coping mechanism. Practice turning to Him instead. As you make this a daily habit, you'll find that relying on Jesus becomes second nature, and His strength will be your constant source of support.

Prayer

Father, thank You for the reminder that just as physical skills require practice, our spiritual connection with You thrives through continuous effort. Grant us the discipline and commitment to seek You in every aspect of our lives. Strengthen our spiritual muscles so encountering your presence becomes second nature. In Jesus' name, we pray. Amen.

Notes

_____

_____

_____

_____

_____

_____

_____

Day 16: God Speaks

Scripture

Isaiah 43:1b - "Fear not, for I have redeemed you; I have called you by name, you are mine."

Reflection

I clearly remember the first time I acknowledged God speaking to me in my spirit. I was getting ready for bed when, out of nowhere, I had this thought in my head that I knew was from the Lord: "I know your name, Emily. I know you. I see you. I created you." The very next day at church, the entire message was about how God knows us by name. I didn't know that was going to be the message, of course, but it was God reminding me that He does know me, He does see me, and He did create me. Not only that, but He is active in my life and wants me to hear His voice when He speaks to me.

And the same is true for you: He knows YOUR name. He created YOU. He is active in YOUR life. He wants to speak to YOU.

Whoever you are reading this, wherever you are on your faith journey, whatever mistakes you have made, know this: Jesus knows your name. He created you. He knows your every thought. He sees where you've been, and He knows exactly where you're going. He has a plan for your life, and it's a good plan. And He is crazy about you! He loves you, unconditionally.

Devotional Message

Consider this: the very Creator of the universe, the one who flung stars into space, knows YOU by name. His concern for you goes beyond the grandeur of galaxies; it's rooted in the details of your life. Imagine the Creator of time and space being deeply invested in every single moment of your existence. He is there when you wake up, when you go to work or school, when you face challenges, and when you celebrate victories. His desire…? To walk with you intimately, not just in some distant future, but right now, in the midst of your everyday life.

So, let this truth echo in your heart – God knows your name, and His love for you is immeasurable. He is pursuing you with relentless passion, longing for a vibrant, personal connection that unfolds in the small, ordinary moments as much as in the big, life-changing ones. Whether you're washing dishes, driving to work, or sitting in silence at the end of a long day, He is with you, and He cares deeply about every aspect of your life.

Reflective Question

How does the understanding that God knows you by name and cares about every detail of your life impact your daily perspective and choices?

Prayer

Lord, thank You for the comforting truth that You know me intimately and care about every aspect of my life. Help me to walk in the awareness of Your presence and to align my choices with Your loving guidance. In Jesus' name, I pray. Amen.

Notes

_____

_____

_____

_____

_____

Day 17: The Band-Aid Faith

Scripture

Matthew 19:14 (NLT) "But Jesus said, 'Let the children come to me. Don't stop them; For the Kingdom of Heaven belongs to those who are like these children.'

Reflection

In the world of my little boys, a Band-Aid is a magical solution—they believe it can fix anything, from a small cut to an imaginary injury. Their unwavering trust in this simple adhesive strip teaches us a profound truth about the faith God desires from us.

Devotional Message

God calls us to approach Him with a childlike trust, similar to my children's unwavering faith in a Band-Aid. As adults, life's complexities often lead us to seek intricate solutions for our problems. We may think we need detailed plans, extensive advice, or complex strategies to navigate our challenges. But God invites us to trust in His simplicity and to rely on Him as a child would.

Think about your own life. What wounds or challenges are you facing right now? Perhaps you're dealing with stress at work, a strained relationship, or financial worries. Maybe you're struggling with feelings of inadequacy or fear of the future. Instead of trying to figure it all out on your own, can you approach God with the unshakable trust of a child reaching for a Band-Aid?

Consider these examples:

- **When anxiety starts to creep in:** Instead of trying to manage it on your own or seeking a complicated solution, simply take a deep breath, say a short prayer, and trust that

God will provide the peace you need in that moment.

- **In moments of decision-making:** Whether it's a big life choice or a daily task, rather than overanalyzing, pause and ask God for guidance. Trust that He will lead you in the right direction, just as a child trusts that a Band-Aid will make everything better.
- **When facing a difficult conversation:** If you're dreading a discussion with someone, approach it with the faith that God will give you the right words and the grace to handle it well, just as a child trusts in the comfort of a Band-Aid to ease their pain.

But this concept goes further than just these examples—it can be applied to every situation we might face in our lives. Trusting God with childlike faith isn't always easy, and it takes practice and intentionality. We might not get it right every time, and that's okay. But the more we intentionally turn to God and trust in His provision, the better we'll get at it over time.

Sometimes, it's the simplicity of faith that allows God to work wonders. Just as a child doesn't doubt the power of a Band-Aid, we're called to believe wholeheartedly in God's ability to heal, guide, and provide. Let the innocence of a child's belief in Band-Aids inspire your unwavering faith in God's miraculous touch. Whatever you're facing, remember that God's love and power are more than enough to handle it, no matter how big or small.

Reflective Question:

What area of your life do you need to hand over to God with childlike trust? How can you start practicing this kind of faith today?

Notes

_____

_____

Day 18: Pursued by Love

Scripture

Matthew 18:12 (NLT) - "If a man has a hundred sheep and one of them wanders away, what will he do? Won't he leave the ninety-nine others on the hills and go out to search for the one that is lost?"

Reflection

The other day, my 4-year-old was visibly upset. When I asked him what was wrong, he hesitated before saying, "I don't want you to be mad!" I realized he was afraid to tell me what he had done wrong because he didn't want to disappoint me. It struck me how often we do the same with God. We make mistakes or stray off course and then fear approaching Him, worried that He might be angry or that we're somehow unworthy of His love.

But just as I reassured my son that I wasn't mad, God reassures us with His boundless love. In Matthew 18:12, Jesus tells the story of a shepherd who leaves the ninety-nine sheep to search for the one that is lost. This isn't a story of condemnation but of pursuit and love. While God isn't happy about our sin because He sees how it destroys us, His desire is for us to turn from it. He's not waiting to punish us but is eager to forgive us if we ask. God doesn't hold grudges or keep a record of our wrongs; instead, He actively seeks us out, ready to welcome us back with open arms and a heart full of grace.

Devotional Message

Reflect on the powerful image of a shepherd leaving the majority to find the one lost sheep. This story illustrates God's relentless pursuit of us, even when we feel lost or distant. Life can be overwhelming, and it's easy to think that we've strayed too far from God's love. But the truth is, God's love isn't conditional or limited by our mistakes. He isn't waiting to scold us; instead, He's longing to help us turn from our sins and restore us to wholeness.

Think about moments when you've felt distant from God—maybe because of guilt, shame, or fear. Perhaps you've hesitated to pray, feeling unworthy or afraid of His response. But here's the truth: God's love for you is greater than any mistake or failure. He's not sitting in judgment, waiting to punish you. Instead, He's longing to bring you back into His embrace and guide you away from what harms you.

Embrace the truth that you are pursued by love, and nothing can separate you from the love of your Heavenly Father. This love isn't just a concept; it's an active force in your life. No matter where you've been or what you've done, God's love remains constant, unwavering, and ready to restore you if you turn to Him.

Reflective Question

Have you ever hesitated to approach God, fearing His anger or disappointment? How does the image of a loving shepherd pursuing a lost sheep change your perspective on God's love for you?

Prayer

Lord, thank You for pursuing me with a love that knows no bounds. Help me embrace the truth that I am pursued by love, and nothing can separate me from Your relentless and unconditional love; may this awareness deepen my relationship with You. Amen.

Notes

_____

_____

_____

Day 19: Vision Beyond Our Own

Scripture

Proverbs 3:5-6 (NLT) - "Trust in the Lord with all your heart; do not depend on your own understanding. Seek His will in all you do, and He will show you which path to take."*

Reflection

The day after my LASIK eye surgery remains vivid in my memory, marked by 24 hours of blurred and unclear vision. Yet, the following day brought perfect clarity. This experience reminds me that sometimes, we must endure challenges to reach the other side, where the path becomes clearer and easier. Just like the post-surgery blur, facing difficulties can be tough, but they are often necessary for the ultimate clarity and improvement we seek.

Devotional Message

Just as my vision was temporarily blurred before becoming clear after LASIK, our lives often go through challenging seasons before we reach a place of clarity and peace. It's like a garden that must be tilled before it can yield beautiful crops—the soil has to be broken and disturbed before it can produce fruit. Similarly, our lives sometimes need to be shaken up before we can see the growth and blessings God has in store for us.

Proverbs 3:5-6 encourages us to trust in the Lord with all our hearts, especially when our understanding is limited. There are times when the work God is doing in our lives feels confusing or even painful. You might be facing a difficult decision, a season of uncertainty, or a struggle that seems overwhelming. In those moments, it's tempting to rely on our own understanding and try to take control, but this often leads to more confusion and frustration.

Instead, God invites us to trust Him completely. Imagine the relief that comes when you finally let go of trying to figure everything out on your own. When you surrender your struggles and uncertainties to Him, He promises to guide you. Just as my vision cleared after the initial blur, God's plan will become clearer in time, revealing a brighter and more purposeful path for your life.

In every part of your life, whether it's the small daily choices or the big life-altering decisions, make it a habit to seek God's will. Even when things seem unclear, trust that He is working behind the scenes to bring about a good outcome. Entrusting God with your struggles allows Him to lead you to a brighter, clearer, and flourishing vision for your life. The process might not always be easy, but just like the clarity I experienced after LASIK, the results will be worth it.

Reflective Question

Reflect on a challenging time in your life that eventually brought about positive change. What growth and clarity emerged through the difficulty?

Prayer

Lord, I trust in Your plan for my life, even when circumstances seem challenging and unclear. Help me understand that difficulties are often part of a process leading to positive change. Guide me through the tough times, knowing You are working for my ultimate good. Amen.

Notes

_____

_____

_____

Day 20: Impossible Made Possible

Scripture

Matthew 19:26 (NLT) - "Jesus looked at them intently and said, 'Humanly speaking, it is impossible. But with God, everything is possible.'"

Reflection

There are moments in life when things seem impossible, and it's easy to lose hope. Yet, our faith teaches us that with God, everything is possible. I was reminded of this in a funny and unexpected way when my husband and brother-in-law faced what seemed like an impossible task: moving a large sectional couch into my mom's home (if you've ever tried this, you know the struggle!). Despite the initial challenges and doubts, they persisted, and to everyone's surprise, the couch found its place—but not without removing two doors from their hinges. It was a small but powerful reminder that sometimes, to make the impossible possible, we have to remove obstacles or change our approach. God often does the same in our lives—He removes barriers, changes circumstances, and makes a way where there seems to be none.

Devotional Message

Think about the moments in your life when you've faced obstacles that seemed insurmountable. Maybe it was a financial crisis, a relationship that was falling apart, or a health scare that felt overwhelming. Just as we had to remove the doors to get that couch into the room, sometimes God has to remove things from our lives to make a way for us. It might be a relationship that's not right for us, a job that's holding us back, or even a mindset that's limiting our faith.

God is always at work, often in ways we don't immediately

recognize. He might close one door to open another, or take something away to give you something even better. These moments might seem challenging or even painful at the time, but they are often God's way of clearing the path for something greater.

Consider how many times you've made it through situations that seemed impossible at first, only to realize later that God had been working behind the scenes all along. Reflect on those times when God's intervention paved a way when you felt hopeless. It's easy to overlook these moments or chalk them up to coincidence, but when we look back, we can see God's hand guiding us through.

Jesus reminds us, "With God, everything is possible." As you navigate life's uncertainties, hold onto the assurance that God is the master of possibilities. When the path seems blocked or the doors seem shut, trust that God is already working to remove obstacles and make a way for you. Just as my husband and brother-in-law removed those doors to fit the couch into the room, God can remove barriers in your life, making the impossible possible.

Remember, God's transformative power extends beyond human understanding. He is always working, often in ways we don't immediately see. Let these reflections fortify your faith, and the next time something "impossible" becomes possible, take a moment to thank God for removing the doors and making a way in your life.

Reflective Question

Can you recall a situation in your life where God made the impossible possible? How did that experience deepen your faith?

Prayer

Lord, thank You for being the God of possibilities. Help me trust in Your power to make a way when things seem impossible. Strengthen my faith and remind me that with You, everything is possible. In Jesus' name, I pray. Amen.

Notes

_____

_____

_____

_____

_____

_____

_____

_____

_____

_____

_____

_____

_____

_____

_____

_____

_____

_____

_____

_____

_____

_____

_____

Emily Hampton

Day 21: Perception vs. Reality

Scripture

Psalm 139:23-24 (NLT) - "Search me, O God, and know my heart; test me and know my anxious thoughts. Point out anything in me offending You, and lead me along the path of everlasting life."

Reflection

Before the birth of my first son, I was an elementary school teacher. I once received feedback from a parent suggesting I lacked compassion. It devastated me because I knew I cared deeply for my students, and I took great pride in my ability to love them well. Thankfully, my administration recognized my caring nature and reassured me that I, in fact, did not lack compassion. Being a sensitive person, I've learned to navigate situations with God's truth and grace. It's a humbling reminder that our actions might be misunderstood by others. In these moments, we can find solace in knowing God intimately understands our hearts.

Devotional Message:

The unforgettable incident with that parent became a profound chapter in my journey, teaching me a lesson that resonates deeply: not everyone will perceive us as we truly are. In those times, we have to ask ourselves, "What does Jesus say about me?" It's a humbling recognition that our sincere efforts to show love and compassion might be veiled by the lens of human misinterpretation.

This experience drew a stark parallel to the reality that even Jesus, in His flawless love, faced profound misunderstanding and judgment. How many people misunderstood the most loving, perfect human to ever walk this Earth? Yet, Jesus continued to love, serve, and fulfill His purpose, trusting in God's understanding rather than human opinions.

In these moments, let our guiding prayer be Psalm 139:23-24. When others question our intentions or misunderstand our actions, we can find strength in God's perception of us, trusting that our earnest efforts are seen and valued by the One who intimately knows our hearts. Like Jesus embraced the cross, we can find assurance that God's perception transcends the veils of human judgment, anchoring us in His eternal love and understanding.

When you find yourself misunderstood or judged unfairly, take a moment to pause and pray, asking God to search your heart. Reflect on Psalm 139:23-24, asking Him to reveal any areas where you might need to grow, but also to remind you of who you are in His eyes. It's important to balance the desire to learn and grow with the understanding that not every criticism reflects the truth of who we are.

Instead of being discouraged, let these moments be an opportunity to draw closer to God, seeking His guidance and reassurance. Ask Him to help you respond with grace and love, even when others don't see your heart. Remember, your worth and identity are rooted in God's love and understanding, not in the opinions of others.

Reflective Question

How can the experiences of Jesus, who faced profound misunderstanding and judgment, inspire and guide you as you navigate moments of misjudgment in your own life?

Prayer

Lord, search my heart, and reveal any areas that need refinement. Help me focus on Your perception of me, trusting that my sincere intentions are known and valued by You. Lead me on the path of everlasting life. In Jesus' name, I pray. Amen.

Grace Like Wildflowers

Notes

_____

_____

_____

_____

_____

_____

_____

_____

_____

_____

_____

_____

_____

_____

_____

_____

_____

_____

_____

_____

_____

_____

_____

_____

_____

Emily Hampton

Day 22: You Know, I'm Not all that Different from a Daisy

Scripture

Luke 15:4-5 (NLT) - "Suppose one of you has a hundred sheep and loses one of them. Doesn't he leave the ninety-nine in the open country and go after the lost sheep until he finds it?"

Reflection

Did you know that daisies are technically weeds? I think that is one of the things that draws me to them-their beauty stands out amongst the other less desirable weeds. I truly believe that Jesus saw me in a similar light-His beautiful, beloved daughter, lost amongst the weeds. In my life, I was growing—but towards the wrong things: selfish ambition, earthly pleasures, popularity, and partying. It wasn't hard to see that I wasn't living the life God intended for me.

Daisies have always been my favorite flower. As I look at them growing in the fields, I'm struck by their beauty despite being labeled as weeds. It reminds me that even when I didn't walk with Jesus, He still saw me as beautiful and worthy. He knew I was a "weed," making poor choice after poor choice, but He was able to look beyond that.

Devotional Message

The more I grew into the wrong things, the more uprooted I felt-my pursuits left me feeling hollow and disconnected, longing for something more. But God's grace and love for His precious children (you and me) is bigger than we can imagine. Just as a daisy's beauty shines through despite being a weed, God sees us as precious and valuable, even in our brokenness. He loves us unconditionally, forgiving our sins and shortcomings when we turn our hearts and lives towards Him.

When I finally turned to God, I realized He had been waiting for me all along, seeing my potential and worth-and yes, even the beauty that I was unable to see in myself. If I'm honest, I didn't think He could ever love a sinner like me, but His love and grace helped me to grow in the right direction, towards the life He had always intended for me: a life pointed towards Him. Not a perfect, sinless life (we all stumble), but a real life marked by the love and grace of the Creator of the World.

Reflective Question

Have you ever considered yourself too lost to be found by God's love? How does the parable of the lost sheep, illustrating God's joy in welcoming back a sinner, transform your view of His grace?

Notes

_____

_____

_____

_____

_____

_____

_____

_____

_____

_____

Day 23: Breaking Free from the Chains of People Pleasing

Scripture

Galatians 1:10 (NLT) - "Obviously, I'm not trying to win the approval of people, but of God. If pleasing people were my goal, I would not be Christ's servant."

Reflection

For much of my life, I found myself entangled in the web of seeking others' approval. Decisions about how to dress, what to say, or even the choices I made in my personal and professional life often hinged on the thoughts and opinions of those around me. I was driven by questions like, "What will they think?" or "How will this affect their perception of me?" It's easy to become ensnared by the desire to fit in or be liked, but this pursuit can overshadow the more important goal of seeking God's approval.

Devotional Message

Galatians 1:10 offers a liberating perspective. The Apostle Paul's message underscores that the approval of others is fleeting and often inconsequential compared to the approval of God. Think about the moments when you've been torn between following your heart and conforming to others' expectations. Maybe it was deciding whether to take a new job that aligned with your passions but seemed unconventional, or perhaps it was speaking up in a situation where it felt safer to remain silent.

These decisions reflect a deeper question: Are we striving to please people or are we focused on pleasing God? When we shift our focus from people-pleasing to seeking God's approval, we find freedom. For instance, imagine a situation where you are tempted to make a choice just to fit in or avoid conflict. By asking yourself, "What would please God in this situation?" you can shift your perspective. Embracing God's approval allows you to be authentic and true to yourself, freeing you from the constraints of others' expectations.

Let's remember, our true worth and approval come from God. When we align our actions with His will, we step into a life marked by authenticity and peace.

Reflective Question

In what areas of your life are you still seeking approval from others? How can you shift your focus to seek God's approval instead?

Prayer

Heavenly Father, liberate me from the chains of people pleasing. Help me seek Your approval above all else, finding freedom in the acceptance and love You offer. Guide my decisions and actions in alignment with Your will. In Jesus' name, I pray. Amen.

Notes

_____

_____

_____

_____

_____

_____

_____

_____

Day 24: Trusting in the Unknown

Scripture

Proverbs 3:5-6 - "Trust in the Lord with all your heart and lean not on your own understanding; in all your ways submit to Him, and He will make your paths straight."

Reflection

When my boys were babies, car rides were a real challenge. Buckling them into their car seats was always a struggle, and their cries often made me question whether there was a better way. Yet, I knew that ensuring their safety and following the rules of car travel were essential, even if they didn't understand it at the time. Despite their discomfort, I remained focused on what was best for them.

In the same way, God's guidance can sometimes feel uncomfortable or confusing. Just as I had a clear understanding of the necessity of those car rides for my children's safety, God sees the bigger picture of our lives. Even when we can't see why things are happening or understand the path we're on, trusting in His wisdom is crucial.

Devotional Message

Reflect on times when you've faced situations that felt uncomfortable or challenging. Perhaps there were decisions or circumstances where the way forward seemed unclear. Just as I had to stay focused on the well-being of my children, God's plans for us are always for our ultimate good, even if they're not immediately apparent.

Consider your current challenges or decisions. Are there areas where you're struggling to trust God fully? It could be a difficult job decision, a relationship issue, or a personal struggle. Embrace the trust Proverbs 3:5-6 calls us to. Acknowledge that while you may not see the full picture, God's guidance is always with you, leading you towards a path that is ultimately for your benefit and growth.

Let this reminder encourage you to place your trust in God, even when the path isn't clear. He is guiding you, making your path straight, and leading you to a place of peace and purpose.

Reflective Question

How can you actively trust God in an area of your life where understanding is currently lacking?

Prayer

Lord, help me to trust in Your wisdom even when I don't fully comprehend Your plans. Give me the courage to surrender the areas of my life where I struggle to understand, knowing You work all things for my good. In Jesus' name, I pray. Amen.

Notes

_____

_____

_____

_____

_____

_____

_____

_____

_____

_____

Day 25: Choosing Love Over All Else

Scripture

1 Corinthians 13:4 (NLT) - "Love is patient and kind. Love is not jealous or boastful or proud or rude. It does not demand its own way. It is not irritable, and it keeps no record of being wronged."

Reflection

If I'm honest, I sometimes struggle to love others as Jesus does. I find myself distancing from people who don't meet my "ideal" friend criteria or getting caught up in comparison. These feelings can lead to missed opportunities for meaningful connections. In these moments, I'm not just missing out on relationships but also stepping away from embodying Jesus's love. Despite my flaws and shortcomings, Jesus loves me unconditionally and calls me to love others in the same way.

Devotional Message

1 Corinthians 13:4 describes a love that is patient, kind, and free from jealousy, pride, and rudeness. This love doesn't demand its own way and keeps no record of wrongs. Imagine how our lives and relationships could transform if we consistently chose this kind of love. It's not always easy, but practicing patience, kindness, and forgiveness can deeply enrich our interactions. This selfless love requires effort and practice, but God gives us daily opportunities to grow in this love.

To help make this love a reality in our lives, consider the following practical examples of how you can actively practice love in your daily interactions:

- **Choosing Kindness Over Criticism**: When tempted to criticize or judge someone, pause and consider how you can offer encouragement or support instead.
- **Forgiving Quickly**: If someone wrongs you, practice letting go of grudges and choosing forgiveness, even if it's difficult.
- **Embracing Differences**: Make an effort to connect with those who differ from you in beliefs, interests, or backgrounds, and appreciate the unique perspectives they bring.

By committing to love as Jesus calls us to, we open ourselves to richer relationships and a deeper understanding of His love. Let this love guide your actions and interactions, and witness how it transforms your heart and relationships.

Reflective Question

Reflect on your own love: Are you patient and kind? Not jealous, boastful, proud, or rude? Do you demand your own way, or are you irritable? Do you keep a record of wrongs, or do you rejoice in the truth? Do you give up, lose faith, or endure through every circumstance?

Prayer

Lord, help me choose love over all else. In moments of difficulty, let me mirror Your unconditional love. Guide me to embody the characteristics of love outlined in 1 Corinthians 13:4. May my choices reflect Your love and bring more friendship, opportunities, and acceptance into my life. Amen.

Grace Like Wildflowers

Notes

_____
_____
_____
_____
_____
_____
_____
_____
_____
_____
_____
_____
_____
_____
_____
_____
_____
_____
_____
_____
_____
_____
_____

Emily Hampton

Day 26: Embracing Imperfections

Scripture

2 Corinthians 12:9 (NLT): "My grace is all you need. My power works best in weakness."

Reflection

This morning, a memory from my teaching days came to mind. I recalled a beautiful moment in my math class when a student made a mistake and looked visibly embarrassed. In that classroom, something truly redeeming happened. Another student, recognizing her classmate's struggle, boldly declared, "Don't feel bad… ME TOO! I also messed up!" What followed was incredible: all around the room, others began speaking up, sharing their own mistakes and times they had answered questions incorrectly. This scene was, to me, the ultimate picture of what living life together should look like: admitting our mistakes, comforting each other, and prioritizing empathy over appearing perfect. It struck me how, as adults, we often try to hide our imperfections to avoid shame.

Devotional

Acknowledging our imperfections isn't a sign of weakness but an invitation to experience God's grace and love more deeply. The brave student's admission created an environment where others felt safe to be vulnerable, embracing imperfection together. In these moments, we have the opportunity to share and fully accept God's grace and love for us. God calls us to be bold and fearless in our walk with Him, embracing our flaws while encouraging one another.

Consider how you can create spaces of acceptance and grace in your own life. Reflect on how you can openly acknowledge your own imperfections and extend comfort to others. By doing so, you embrace the true essence of community and experience the depth of God's love in the process.

Reflective Question

Reflect on a recent situation where you felt the need to hide imperfections. How might embracing those imperfections have created a space for God's grace and love?

Prayer

Lord, give me the courage to embrace imperfections and live fearlessly in Your love. Help me recognize moments to share vulnerability, creating space for Your grace to work in my life and the lives of those around me. Thank You for your never-ending love and understanding. Amen.

Notes

_____

_____

_____

_____

_____

_____

_____

_____

_____

_____

_____

Day 27: God's Loving Delight

Scripture

Matthew 7:11 (NIV) - "If you, then, though you are evil, know how to give good gifts to your children, how much more will your Father in heaven give good gifts to those who ask Him!"

Reflection

As a parent, I've had the sheer delight of watching my kids play a claw machine game, their eyes brimming with anticipation and hope. I found myself holding my breath, secretly rooting for them to grasp that coveted prize – a small but precious joy. In those moments, I was struck by how God, our loving Father, delights in giving us good things, much like I do with my children.

Devotional Message

Our heavenly Father's love for us is immeasurable, and His desire to bless us is boundless. Just as I hope with all my heart for my children to experience joy and success, God's heart longs to see us embrace the blessings He has in store for us. He watches over us with loving anticipation, eager to bestow gifts that go beyond material possessions – gifts of love, grace, peace, and purpose. Imagine God, as a loving Father, holding His breath in anticipation, eager to grant you the good gifts that bring true joy and fulfillment. As you go through your day, consider the desires of your heart and approach God with your hopes and dreams, trusting in His unwavering love and His commitment to providing for His children.

Reflective Question

What are the desires of your heart that you can bring before God today, trusting in His loving desire to give you good gifts?

Prayer

Heavenly Father, thank You for being a loving and generous parent. I bring my hopes, dreams, and desires before You, trusting in Your goodness; may I experience the joy of receiving the good gifts You have prepared for me. Amen.

Notes

_____
_____
_____
_____
_____
_____
_____
_____
_____
_____
_____
_____
_____
_____

Day 28: Unveiling Hidden Healing

Scripture

Isaiah 55:8-10 NLT – "'My thoughts are nothing like your thoughts,' says the LORD. 'And my ways are far beyond anything you could imagine.'"

Reflection

Have you ever had one of those days where everything feels off? Maybe it's something small, like waking up with a slight headache or noticing that your favorite shirt has a stain. You brush it off, thinking it's no big deal. But as the day goes on, that headache gets worse, or that stain seems to grow, and suddenly you're dealing with something more serious than you expected. It's a reminder that sometimes what starts as a minor issue can turn into something that demands your full attention.

This reminds me of when my son was four years old. He started complaining about a bellyache, and we didn't think much of it at first. Maybe he ate too much candy or was coming down with a bug. But as the hours passed, his discomfort grew, and we realized this wasn't something that would just go away. It turned out to be appendicitis, a serious condition that required immediate surgery. What seemed minor at first was actually a sign of something much deeper that needed to be addressed.

Devotional Message

In our lives, we often encounter situations that seem small or insignificant—like a disagreement with a friend, a tough day at work, or a lingering feeling of unease. It's easy to shrug these things off, thinking they'll resolve on their own. But sometimes, these small issues are signals that something deeper is going on, something that God wants us to notice and address.

God's perspective is different from ours. He sees the bigger picture and knows what's truly at the root of our struggles. What might seem like a minor inconvenience to us could be God's way of gently nudging us to pay attention, to dig deeper, and to seek His guidance. Just like my son's bellyache was a warning sign of a more serious condition, the small struggles in our lives can be God's way of inviting us to come to Him, to let Him reveal what needs healing or change.

So, the next time you're dealing with something that seems small but persistent, take a moment to pause and ask God what He might be trying to show you. It could be that He's using this situation to bring you closer to Him, to help you grow, or to lead you to a place of deeper healing. Trust that His ways are always for your good, even when they don't make sense at first.

Reflective Question

Is there something in your life that you've been dismissing as minor, but it keeps coming back? How might God be using this situation to draw you closer to Him or to prompt you to address something deeper?

Notes

_____

_____

_____

_____

_____

_____

Day 29: Overcoming Snow-Covered Stairs

Scripture

Isaiah 43:2 (NLT) - "When you go through deep waters, I will be with you."

Reflection

Stairs have always been a challenge for me. My mom loves to joke about how many times I tripped while climbing our stairs as a child. I vividly remember falling down them in front of my whole college class on my first week of school, stumbling up them through the snow to my first apartment, and many other unfortunate encounters. Despite these hurdles, stairs have also been a vital part of my life. Avoiding them entirely would be impossible and would mean missing out on so many meaningful experiences—like walking up the steps to an arena to watch Monster Jam with my kids, climbing into a pool with them for a summer swim, or simply entering my home.

Devotional Message

In life, we all face our own metaphorical stairs—challenges and obstacles that seem daunting or overwhelming. These might include fighting through body image issues, where the journey to self-acceptance feels like an endless climb, or managing the stress and demands of a difficult job, which can feel like a steep ascent with no clear end. Health problems, whether personal or affecting a loved one, can be like scaling a mountain, and financial struggles might feel like climbing a never-ending staircase. Just as I've learned to navigate stairs in my life, you don't have to face your challenges alone. God promises to be with you through every step of your journey. He'll hold your hand and guide you, providing strength and support when you need it most. Remember that while the stairs may be difficult, they also lead to important and rewarding places. Trust in His presence and keep moving forward, knowing that each step is part of a greater plan.

Reflective Question

What are the metaphorical stairs in your life, and how can remembering that God is with you help you overcome them?

Prayer

Lord, as I navigate life's challenging stairs, both literal and metaphorical, I find comfort in Your promise to be with me through deep waters. Grant me the strength to persevere, knowing that blessings and treasures wait on the other side; may love, joy, and fulfillment be my rewards, as I continue to press forward. Amen.

Notes

_____
_____
_____
_____
_____
_____
_____
_____
_____
_____
_____

Day 30: Unending Grace

Scripture

Ephesians 2:8-9 (NLT) - "God saved you by His grace when you believed. And you can't take credit for this; it is a gift from God. Salvation is not a reward for the good things we have done, so none of us can boast."

Reflection

As we conclude this 30-day journey, let's reflect on the essence of God's grace. Grace, a gift freely given, saved us when we believed. It's not based on our merits; it's God's unearned favor. Through various stories, we've explored the unfolding of grace in our lives - brokenness turning into beauty, imperfections embraced, and freedom from self-imposed cages. Just as God did not ask us to earn His grace, let's extend the same to ourselves and others.

Devotional Message

This journey has been a testament to God's unmerited favor. His grace redeems our imperfections and turns our brokenness into something beautiful. Each day, we've uncovered new facets of His grace - from facing fears to embracing vulnerability. It's a reminder salvation is a gift, not a reward for our deeds. As we close this chapter, let's hold onto the truth that God's grace is enough. Reflect on the stories shared, the challenges faced, and the victories won. Just as God lavishly pours out His grace on us, let's extend grace to ourselves and those around us.

Reflective Question

In what ways have you personally experienced God's grace throughout this journey, and how can you extend that grace to others?

Prayer

Lord, thank You for the gift of grace. As we conclude this journey, help us internalize the truth that Your grace is sufficient; may we extend the same grace to ourselves and others, recognizing that salvation is a gift from You. In Jesus' name, we pray. Amen.

Notes

_____

_____

_____

_____

_____

_____

_____

_____

_____

_____

_____

_____

_____

_____

_____

_____

_____

_____

Bonus Days

Embracing Relationship over Religion

Scripture

Matthew 22:37-39 - Jesus replied, "'You must love the LORD your God with all your heart, all your soul, and all your mind.' This is the first and greatest commandment."

Reflection

Growing up, I was surrounded by religious practices and teachings. Attending a private school meant frequent masses and lessons about God. However, it wasn't until much later that I understood the difference between merely practicing religion and truly cultivating a personal relationship with God. This realization is not uncommon—many of us learn about God without fully grasping His desire for a deep, personal connection.

Devotional Message

Cultivating a relationship with God involves more than following religious rituals; it's about engaging with Him on a personal level. Start by inviting God into your daily routine. Begin each day with a moment of prayer, seeking His guidance and thanking Him for His presence. Integrate small, intentional moments with God throughout your day—whether it's listening to worship music while you work, taking a few quiet minutes to reflect on His word, or sharing your thoughts and feelings with Him during a walk.

Consider how you can make your interaction with God a natural part of your daily life. Instead of viewing prayer and worship as duties, see them as opportunities to connect with a loving Father who is eager to listen and guide you. Embrace His presence in both the joys and challenges of your day-to-day experiences. By doing so, you'll find that your relationship with God becomes more vibrant and meaningful, moving beyond routine into a genuine, heartfelt connection.

Reflective Question

How can you integrate moments of connection with God into your daily life, making your relationship with Him more personal and engaging?

Notes

_____

_____

_____

_____

_____

_____

_____

_____

_____

_____

_____

_____

_____

_____

Open Cage, Soaring Spirit

Scripture

2 Corinthians 3:17 (NLT) - "For the Lord is the Spirit, and wherever the Spirit of the Lord is, there is freedom."

Reflection

Picture a bird trapped in a cage for most of its life. When the door swings open, the bird is set free to soar into the vast sky. Similarly, as I've been writing this book, I've faced moments of self-doubt. Instead of remaining in the cage of fear, I chose to lean on God, trusting Him and walking in the freedom He offers.

Devotional Message

In the early stages of writing this book, self-doubt crept in. Thoughts like "I'm not a theologian" or "Who would want to read what I wrote?" tried to confine me (have you ever had thoughts like these?). These were lies from the enemy. Choosing to listen to God, I heard His reminder: "Emily, you know Me. You walk with Me, deeply love Me, and have experienced My grace. You have all you need to share My love with others." God has opened the door to our cages, offering the greatest freedom imaginable. Like the bird released into the world, we have the vastness of His love and grace to experience. The door is open; freedom awaits you. The choice is ours - to boldly fly into the offered freedom or stay confined in the comfort of our limited world. Acknowledge the open door God has provided for you. Have the courage to accept the love and grace freely given, breaking free from self-imposed limitations. Embrace the freedom that comes from flying into the vastness of God's love.

Reflective Question

What self-imposed limitations or cages are holding you back from fully embracing the freedom God offers?

Prayer

Lord, thank You for opening the door to freedom. Help me find the courage to break free from self-doubt and embrace the love and grace You freely offer. May I soar into the vastness of Your love and experience the freedom You provide. Amen.

Notes

_____

_____

_____

_____

_____

_____

_____

_____

_____

_____

_____

_____

_____

Summary and Thank You to Readers

As we conclude this journey through *Grace Like Wildflowers*, I want to extend a heartfelt thank you to each of you who took the time to read these reflections. Sharing these personal stories and lessons has been a vulnerable experience for me, but I felt deeply called to do so. It has been an honor to open up about the ways grace has blossomed in my life, much like wildflowers emerging in unexpected places.

Just as wildflowers bring beauty and hope to even the most barren landscapes, I hope these reflections have illuminated the grace and love that can be found in the midst of our everyday lives. Each chapter was crafted with the intention of encouraging you to see the divine presence in your own struggles and triumphs, and to cultivate a relationship with God that is as vibrant and authentic as a field of wildflowers.

Thank you for allowing these words into your hearts and minds. I am excited to share that more books are on the way, and I hope you'll join me on future journeys of faith and discovery. May you continue to find grace in the most unexpected places, and may your life be filled with the beauty of wildflowers.

With gratitude and anticipation,

Emily Hampton

www.advbookstore.com

Made in the USA
Columbia, SC
13 December 2024

49186881R00048